SHINE

Brian Lawrence

DEDICATION

Dear Nuri Elise,
Let your energy,individuality, and passion shine your path to greatness.

Love Daddy

Nuri Elise

You are the light of the world. A town built on a hill cannot be hidden. Neither do people light a lamp and put it under a bowl. Instead they put it on its stand, and it gives light to everyone in the house. In the same way, let your light shine before others, that they may see your good deeds and glorify your Father in heaven.

Matthew 5:14-16

Black child God has gifted you a unique light for all the world to see

Let your light shine so you can become who you are divinely called to be

ck child you must shine because lives depend on receiving
ur light
d to reach those who need your radiance you will have to
ne bright

...ne black child shine when you pursue education

...od grades are expected but scholarship should be your

...mary motivation

ne black child shine when you explore leadership in your
mmunity

t your light shine brightest on injustice and fostering unity

ne black child shine when you choose the members of your
ck

ur friends should help you fly higher not weigh you down like
eavy rock

ne black child shine as your glow must reach your brothers
d sisters
ow them love, respect, and appreciation and they will become
r greatest assisters

he black child shine and try your best when you compete

erstand there are lessons to be learned even in defeat

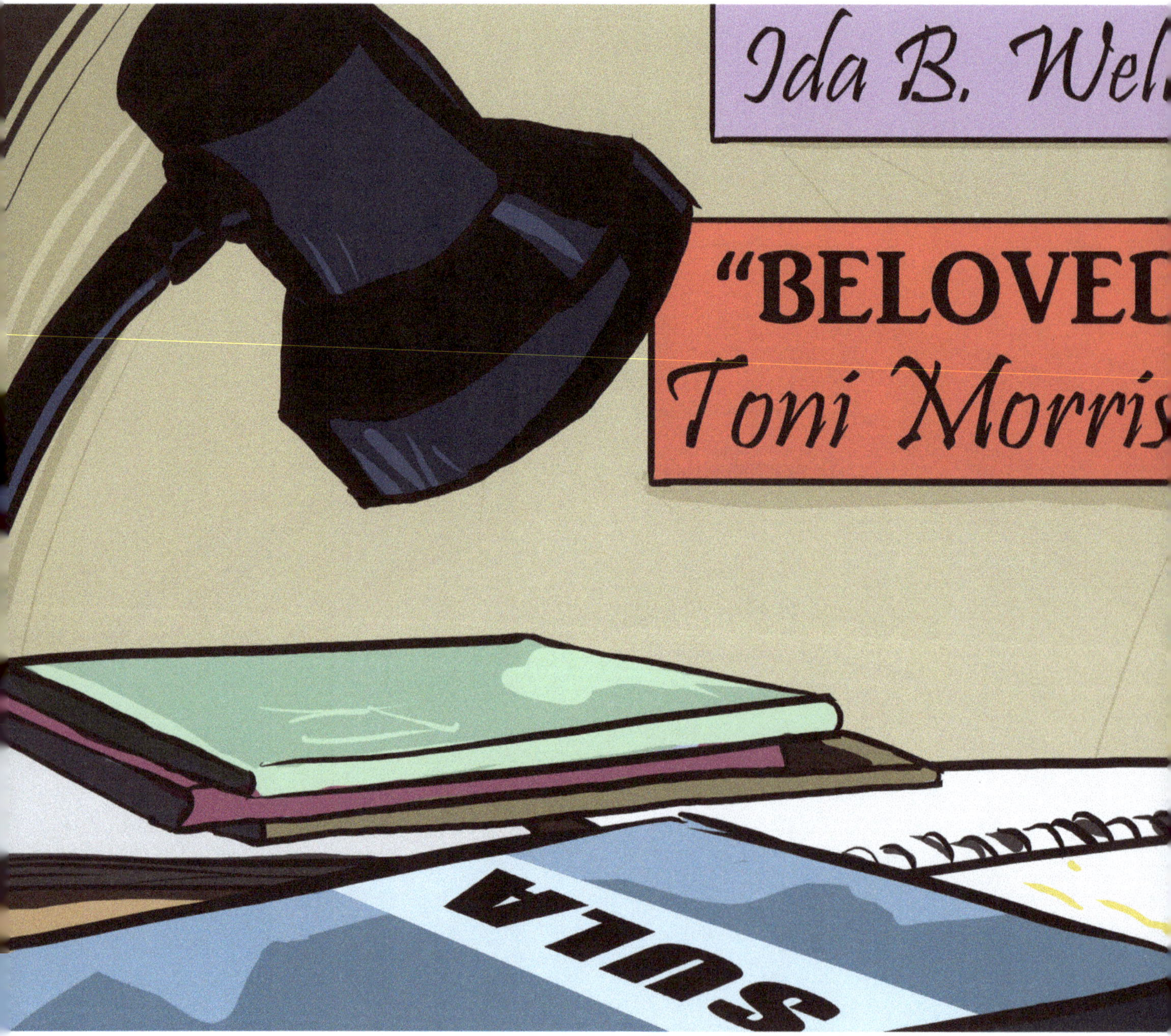
Ida B. Wel
“BELOVED
Toni Morris
SULA

shine like Toni Morrison, Langston Hughes, and Ida B. Wells

as the power of the pen that helped them learn where their

t dwelled

ne like

ricia Bath, Betty Harris, and Ernest Just

through the lens of science their lights were thrust

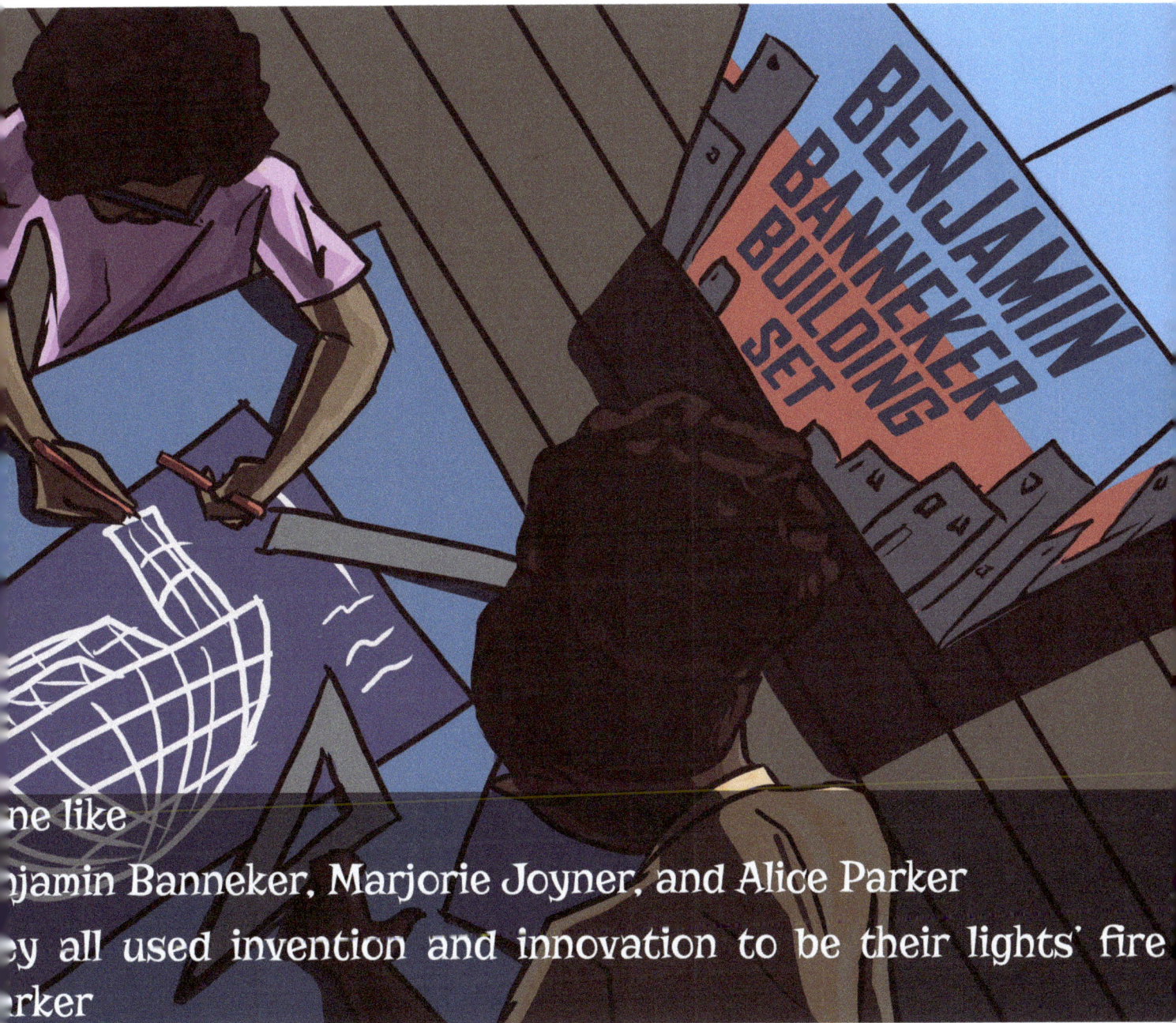

BEN JAMIN BANNEKER BUILDING SET

...ne like

...njamin Banneker, Marjorie Joyner, and Alice Parker

...y all used invention and innovation to be their lights' fire

...rker

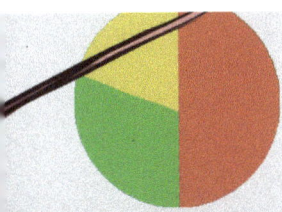

*TECHNOLOGY
*REAL ESTATE
*PHILANTHROPY

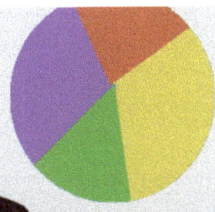

...ne like
...rah Winfrey, Bob Johnson, and Cathy Hughes
...ese people-built empires betting on themselves as if they had
...hing to lose

...ne like

...ena, Magic, and Flojo

...o shined so brightly in sports their last names you don't have

...now

nally, black child remember your existence is divine
ways be one after GOD'S own heart and let your light SHINE
HINE SHINE!

About the Author

Brian's creativity is largely informed by the responsibility he feels to make content that promotes literacy, helps build self-esteem and encourages cultural awareness. Any project that has his name on it will inspire people of color and help them embrace their individuality, strengthen their talents and stimulate cultural pride.

www.ingramcontent.com/pod-product-compliance
Lightning Source LLC
Chambersburg PA
CBHW040252100426
42811CB00011B/1237